THE
WASTELAND

THE WASTELAND

A POETIC NOVEL

GORDON BOSTIC

PRIMIX
PUBLISHING
THE WRITE CHOICE

Primix Publishing
East Brunswick Office Evolution
1 Tower Center Boulevard, Ste 1510
East Brunswick, NJ 08816
www.primixpublishing.com
Phone: 1-800-538-5788

Published by Primix Publishing: 11/26/2025

ISBN: 979-8-89194-573-9(sc)
ISBN: 979-8-89194-574-6(e)

Library of Congress Control Number: 2025925229

Any people depicted in stock imagery provided by iStock are models,
and such images are being used for illustrative purposes only.

Certain stock imagery © iStock.

*For my wonderful wife, Susan
and her loving, adoptive parents,
Al and Ann.*

CONTENTS

THE WASTELAND

All believed it was a wasteland
Where few would venture in.
For those who had proved brave enough
Were never seen again.

The product of an all-out war
That should not have occurred.
But there were egomaniacs
Who could not be deterred.

A place where life could not succeed
Nor nurture would provide.
For the Wasteland had been barren
As all within had died.

Even pets would shun the Wasteland
As if they somehow knew
That the Wasteland had posed a threat
That they would not pursue.

It was left as a reminder
How foolish man could be.
Who left behind a worthless tract
For all eternity.

THE TOWN OF WINSTON

The town of Winston stood outside
The Wasteland borderline.
It had a jaded history
That many would malign.

Although the facts had been obscured
What most seemed to believe
There were remnants from the Wasteland
That had refused to leave.

Where the town they reconstructed
Was to match what they lost.
Though they claimed was not a tribute
To line that had been crossed.

It pretty much was self-contained
Where visitors were few.
Their pride was self-sufficiency
A fact that they clung to.

They'd little contact with the world
Just as they had preferred.
The world had once abandoned them
Where anger was incurred.

SCOTT AND ELIZABETH EVANS

Scott was an army veteran
Who proudly served two tours.
He met his wife on his return
Where his life faced detours.

Scott's wife's name was Elizabeth,
Though he had called her Liz.
She left Winston to go to school
As she proved a math whiz.

Though they had met by accident,
It was love at first sight.
They'd only dated a few months
When timing he thought right.

He entered the Academy
On day of his discharge.
Where upon his graduation
Winston assigned his charge.

For Liz it was a homecoming
As she'd been gone for years.
But for him a new beginning
As he had changed careers.

While the couple had been childless,
They're not lost to despair.
For they hoped for a miracle
As they'd express in prayer.

They were thinking of adoption
But that had been denied.
They thought his job too dangerous
Where caution had applied.

John McGuire

The only one who'd speak to him
Was Trooper John McGuire.
He, too, had been an outsider
Who had stirred people's ire.

No roots to the community
Had made suspicions rise.
Where his motives had been questioned
With doubts quick to arise.

They met at the Academy
And quickly became friends.
But neither one would ever guess
Through assignment extends.

They supported one another
To have each other's back.
For they knew at any moment
They could face an attack.

The other troopers had denied
That trust had been withheld.
But it was more than evident
They wanted each expelled.

THE ELDER

The elder of the town had been
A man known as John Smith.
They claimed that he was ninety-one
Though he would claim the fifth.

While they'd look to him for answers,
Few answers he'd provide.
Though he had a wealth of knowledge
It seemed that most he'd hide.

While his father was a founder
Much knowledge he possessed.
Unlike the other citizens
Most of it was repressed.

He would refuse to speak of it
As all of them were scarred.
Results of war were absolute
And many of them marred.

All in town knew he kept secrets
But figured he was due.
Because he seemed a tortured soul
From everything he knew.

THE RETURN

Elizabeth was welcomed home
While Scott had been ignored.
Elizabeth was prodigal
While Scott's past unexplored.

Although Scott was a State Trooper
No trust had he deserved.
For to them he was a stranger
Where acceptance reserved.

Her parents long since passed away
But home was hers to own.
With Winston as his assignment
To them it had been thrown.

Yet, no neighbors had welcomed them
Nor introductions made.
In fact, their presence was ignored
As though people afraid.

Liz said they would warm up to them
If given enough time.
But was not sure when that may be
Though hoped in their lifetime.

THE GIRL FROM THE WASTELAND

It's from the Wasteland she emerged
Lacking identity.
She seemed a stranger to the land
As if lost entity.

Scott Evans was a State Trooper
Who came across the girl.
She'd seemed to wander aimlessly
As mind had seemed to swirl.

For she seemed disoriented
As though she was confused.
He stopped to see if he could help
In fear she'd been abused.

He found she had been barely clothed
As tatters she had worn.
Thus, he offered her his jacket
But look returned was scorn.

He inquired as to her address
And asked her for her name.
But no reply was forthcoming
As nothing would she claim.

To find out where she had come from
And name would be pursued,
He took the girl to his barracks
Where she'd be interviewed.

THE INTERVIEW

The girl seemed truly hesitant
To separate from Scott
When others had tried to lead her
Their hands the girl would swat.

But, finally, she relinquished
When Scott nodded okay.
Though she'd glance over her shoulder
As they led her away.

She at first was unresponsive
To questions that were asked.
As though the answers she withheld
Or needed to be masked.

Some thought the girl was autistic
As she would not respond.
She simply would just stare ahead
And would not correspond.

She appeared to be seventeen
But none could know for sure.
For without cooperation
No info could secure.

THE INTERROGATION

Scott's superiors questioned him
To where the girl was found.
Which Scott had thought was curious
If not a bit profound.

Scott replied outside the Wasteland,
About two miles from town.
She wandered rather aimlessly
But had not flagged him down.

She seemed to be a wounded waif
Who was lost and alone.
For she came with no possessions
Nor nothing seemed to own.

They asked how long he had known her
As to him she'd seemed drawn.
He repeated he had found her
That morning after dawn.

They asked about her state of dress
As she was almost nude.
Scott replied the way he found her
But thought he may be screwed.

That's why he gave her his jacket
To modesty reclaim.
Though she had not seemed to notice
Showing no signs of shame.

It seemed an interrogation
Which he had undergone.
As if feared he's hiding something
Or facts he had withdrawn.

Scott found it more than curious
Such int'rest had been shown
In an apparent runaway
Whose name had been unknown.

A NEW HOME

When Social Service had been called
The girl had grown alarmed.
More strange people surrounded her
With fear she may be harmed.

When they had tried to restrain her
She'd fought and broken free.
While they'd no wish to harm the girl,
They'd make no guarantee.

They'd not known if she's dangerous
Or to them posed a threat.
But posture said a warrior
As she had been upset.

She'd grabbed a letter opener
She'd brandish with disdain.
It's obvious she would resist
Which she'd made very plain.

When Scott had walked into the room
To see what had occurred.
He calmly had walked to her
As threat he had deterred.

She handed him the opener
As, clearly, she stood down.
"Perhaps," Scott said, "it may be best
If he took her to town."

She could stay with Scott and his wife
Where safety was assured.
They'd give her some stability
From what she had endured.

Perhaps if she had felt secure
Her secrets she'd reveal.
Then, maybe, she would open up
To answer their appeal.

THE WEIGHT

When they pulled into the driveway
Scott asked the girl to wait.
His wife he felt he must address
So, he'd lessen his weight.

Before he introduced the girl
Scott thought that Liz should know
His tours of duty weighed on him,
Though hoped it did not show.

Scott never had confessed to Liz
The horrors he had seen.
For he served within a war zone
Where nothing had been clean.

The children he had seen displaced,
Or those tortured or killed
In nightmares would return to him
And still had left him chilled.

He had no wish to worry her
But Liz must understand
He could not let another child
To those horrors withstand.

That's why he took a shine to her
As she, he wished to save.
At least, until a home was found
Or options were less grave.

THE WELCOMING

Liz welcomed her with open arms
Then saw that she was fed.
She searched around to find her clothes
And made up the guest bed.

Liz tried to make her feel at home
For as long as she stayed.
Liz knew it was not permanent
But the time would not trade.

The girl seemed to be overwhelmed
With what was offered her.
She bounced around upon the bed
As though joy to confer.

Tomorrow she'd take her shopping
To buy her some new clothes.
She would not buy her anything
Unless the ones she chose.

THE SHOPPING SPREE

Winston did not have many stores
But they stopped at each one.
The girl seemed to enjoy herself
And Liz was having fun.

Then Liz noticed the icy stares
The two of them received.
As though the two had posed a threat
That people had perceived.

She could see them sharing whispers.
The way that rumors start.
All eyes had seemed to follow them
As though their moves they'd chart.

While neither of them were approached,
The stares had said it all.
As though they were an oddity
Which had made Liz feel small.

The girl had seemed oblivious
Which Liz was thankful for.
For she had seen enough trauma
And had no need of more.

THE OTHER TROOPERS

Scott had found the other troopers
Had all seemed to avoid
Engaging in conversation
As all had seemed annoyed.

He was not sure what he had done
To piss off everyone.
But it had been made plain to him
That with him they were done.

It seemed to happen overnight
Which to him had seemed strange.
For he had not worked the night shift
Though glances they'd exchange.

There're rumors Scott abused the girl
Before he brought her in.
That was why she seemed so clingy,
At least, that was the spin.

Interrogation proved to them
That Scott did something wrong.
Where a petition had been signed
That Scott did not belong.

While none directly challenged Scott,
He'd been left in the dark
Of accusations that were made
And rumors they were spark.

THE STIR

Her mystery of appearance
In town had caused a stir.
When Liz told Scott what had occurred
In how they had viewed her.

Scott told Liz it had not been her
But, more likely, the girl.
It was a small community
Where rumors tend to swirl.

He told her the other troopers
Gave him the cold shoulder.
Though it was not made clear to him
Why disdain would smolder.

She knew the town despised strangers,
Which the girl would be one.
It may take an extended time
Before their trust was won.

They'd protect her the best they could
And home they would provide.
They'd not known about the rumors
That had spread far and wide.

THE RUMORS

When Liz heard the dirty rumors,
She knew they were untrue.
But there was no convincing them
That they possessed no clue.

For they'd taken out of context
What truly had occurred.
From a little bit of knowledge
The rumors were inferred.

Although there'd been no evidence
That would support the claim.
None had shown a hesitation
To sully Evans' name.

Liz thankful the girl unaware
Of what Scott was accused.
Though none had focused on the fact
Charges had been refused.

Liz hoped the rumors would die down
In just a day or two.
Believing there'd be someone else
Who rumors would be due.

SOME REGRETS

Although her parents both were dead
Neither one had she missed.
For neither had supported her,
Thus, both she had dismissed.

She'd not been there for either one
Which Liz came to regret.
For it had left her with issues
That she could not reset.

She never felt that she was loved
Nor if they even cared
To support her aspirations
Or worried how she fared.

For a hug was something special
That rarely was bestowed.
While conveying that they loved her
A debt they never owed.

Liz swore if she should get the chance
To raise a child one day.
She'd not follow in their footprints
To parent in their way.

Her child would know that it was loved
In no uncertain terms.
Where there'd never be a question
Nor act that not confirms.

A NAME

They had to find a name for her
Even if they must choose.
They could not keep calling her girl.
As that Scott can't excuse.

It must be one that she'd accept
As Scott would not impose
A name on her she did not like
Or to it would oppose.

Liz read to her a list of names
That she and Scott composed.
She told her to just let them know
If liked one they proposed.

Scott's patience had been growing thin
As each name had been read.
It seemed none had caught her fancy
Where he may bang his head.

Then Liz had read the name of Gwen
Which brought the girl a smile.
Where Scott declared it's decided
Though it had took a while.

GWEN'S KNOWLEDGE
OF THE RUMORS

Gwen had known about the rumors
And of what Scott accused.
She thought it was ridiculous
As she was not abused.

But the truth seemed unimportant
With accusations thrown.
Where rumors based on assumptions
With facts had not been known.

It seemed the kindness Scott had shown
Had, somehow, been a flaw.
As if it had been undeserved
Or was against the law.

The pettiness had surprised her
Where good men put to shame.
For the rumors were disgraceful
With what they chose to claim.

THE STORIES

The Wasteland wrapped in mystery
More than it should have been.
Though there'd been no explanation
To see what laid within.

Although the strange occurrences
Had never been confirmed.
There's no one who had lived in town
That had not them affirmed.

Although Scott not a native son
The stories he had heard.
Which spoke of strange occurrences
That in there had occurred.

There had been stories of strange lights
That sometimes could be seen
Which emitted from the Wasteland
Though had not been routine.

There were tales people saw movement
At either dusk or dawn.
But no features discernable
So, no conclusions drawn.

Elizabeth grew up in town
But said she had no clue.
The stories she had also heard
But never thought them true.

And, yet, the stories still persist
As those in town believed
There was something in the Wasteland
That had been unperceived.

WHY TAKEN IN

Although Gwen was truly grateful
Scott and Liz took her in.
She found that she was curious
What reason may have been.

As a stranger to charity
She found she was confused.
It was clear it was an option
That could have been refused.

While she'd known nothing about them,
She chose to go with Scott.
He could have been a predator
Though, thankfully, was not.

It seemed a stretch to have believed
To kindness they'd concede.
She wondered if they had been paid
Where it was done for greed.

While she saw they had no children,
Was that her role to fill?
Perhaps she had been an option,
So, a dream they'd fulfill.

Though they'd, yet, gave her a reason
Where she would come to doubt
That it's through true sincerity
They wished to help her out.

THE DOUBTERS

Scott never felt as close to Liz
As when Gwen had moved in.
For now, they were a family
Which had been a win-win.

The townsfolk had been mortified
Why Gwen was taken in.
For they'd known nothing about her
Nor who she may have been.

The townsfolk found it scandalous
That Scott's wife would agree
To taking in a teenage girl
Which was a recipe

For undignified behavior
Like they'd seen on TV.
Where the girl may try seduce him
As there's no guarantee.

They had not been blood relatives
So, who's to say for sure
That what goes on behind closed doors
Is innocent and pure?

The questions never went away
Nor doubts would ever fade.
As long as Gwen should live with them
It'd be the price they paid.

THE INCURSIONS

It was said there were incursions
That happened late at night.
Where supplies they said were stolen
Then thieves would take to flight.

Although no one was ever harmed,
It still had been a crime.
Even if the things they'd taken
Had been nickle and dime.

Why the thefts rarely reported
Had seemed a mystery.
Most people would be furious
But they'd not seemed to be.

As though thefts were tolerated
Which truly made no sense.
For someone was responsible
In covering expense.

ACCEPTANCE DENIED

Though the rumors had subsided,
Acceptance was denied.
For Scott was not a native son
So, trust had not applied.

The rumors never truly quelled
As doubts seemed to persist.
Although he'd not been ostracized,
Friendships did not exist.

Most of the troopers were home-grown
Which Scott had thought was strange.
For normally they were dispersed
To cover a wide range.

Perhaps because they're close knitted
He'd been on the outside.
For many of them childhood friends
To whom they each were tied.

Liz warned him it would be like this,
But said if given time
When they'd truly come to know him
Their friendship would be prime.

THE CLAIM

A man rushed into the barracks
Who clearly was alarmed.
He claimed his daughter was missing
And he feared had been harmed.

He said sometimes she'd get confused
Where she'd wander away.
Then he said he had not seen her
Forever and a day.

The Sargent at the desk had asked
If daughter he'd describe.
For they had found a wayward girl
Whose life could not transcribe

The description seemed pretty close
To girl that Scott had found.
But the Sargent grew curious
Why now he'd come around.

Scott found the girl some days ago
But father now shows up?
While he found the claim suspicious,
Not on the up-and-up.

But he could not deny the man
The opportunity
To meet the lost girl face-to-face
And prove identity.

The Sargent placed a call to Scott
To say they may have found
One of the lost girl's family
Who just had come around.

ATTEMPTED ABDUCTION

When Scott told Liz what he had heard,
Liz said she understood.
Then she gave Gwen one final hug
As sometimes crying's good.

As they pulled up to the barracks,
Scott said he had good news.
A fam'ly member had been found
Which had left Gwen to muse.

While Gwen appeared to be happy
Living with Liz and Scott.
So, Scott had felt truly guilty
He'd put her on the spot.

For as soon as she saw the man,
Her impulse was to run.
Scott saw the terror in her eyes
And damned what he had done.

As the man tried to approach Gwen
Scott chose to intercede.
He thought the man may be a fraud
So, Gwen he'd not concede.

The man had seen the jig was up
As he had turned to run.
While Scott had chosen to pursue
He forgot he'd no gun.

The Sargent chose to stay with Gwen
In case the man returned.
Which may mean that Scott was injured
Thus, the Sargent concerned.

The man had simply disappeared
As he made his escape.
Where Scott could only stand and stare
With his mouth left to gape.

When Scott returned Gwen ran to him
Where she had hugged him tight..
The Sargent simply stared and smiled
As scene one of delight.

They had no clue to who he was
That tried to abduct Gwen.
Nor did they know the reason why
So, he may come again.

It added to the mystery
That had surrounded Gwen.
For they still had no idea
To who she may have been.

WHY TAKE THE RISK?

Scott had found that he was livid
With what had just occurred.
Someone had tried abducting Gwen,
Though that he had deterred.

What Scott had felt was biblical
So great had been his rage.
The attempt had been audacious
In how he chose to stage.

It's clear some knowledge of the girl
He, clearly, had possessed.
For the description was too good
To simply have been guessed.

Which had brought to mind the question
What would he want with Gwen?
To Scott she had seemed innocent
Both outside and within.

Even the Sargent was perplexed
With what had just occurred.
The man dared to risk everything
Which truly seemed absurd

What was it that the man had wished
That he'd risk all for Gwen?
What value did she truly have
That he would go all-in.

GWEN FACING JEOPARDY

Liz had stared in shocked amazement
To see they both returned.
She thought that Gwen was gone for good
So, she had grown concerned.

Gwen had run to Liz had hugged her
Before she raced inside.
As Liz had turned to confront Scott
Where truth he best not hide.

When Scott relayed what had occurred
Her face turned ashen white.
What was it that the man desired
Where he caused Gwen such fright?

Scott said that all he knew for sure
Was someone wanted Gwen.
And seemed that they'd do anything
To see that's she's reeled in.

So, both of them must be on guard
With choices that they made.
For Gwen had been in jeopardy
Which both must try evade.

THE HAND OF PROVIDENCE

Each night Liz would engage with Gwen
Before Gwen went to bed.
Who wanted to impress on her
That to them she was led.

Liz thought it had been providence
That had led Scott to her.
For he was simply on patrol
When event would occur.

Who knew if it was someone else
What outcome may have been?
So, it seemed truly fortunate
It's Scott who she'd run-in.

As long as Gwen had wished to stay
Their home would be her home.
And promised her security
Where she'd no need to roam.

It was the hand of providence
That had brought her to them
And they would never turn her out
Nor acts choose to condemn.

They always would be there for her
As long as Gwen had need.
So, she should never hesitate
To ever her case plead.

THE STRANGERS

Liz had noticed there were strangers
Who were watching their house.
Although Liz found it unnerving
She did not tell her spouse.

She had no wish to worry Scott
On chance she had been wrong.
An explanation they may have
To why they'd come along.

Just recently she noticed them,
As she came to recall.
After the barracks incident
When plot Scott would forestall.

It was clear that facts were hidden
As no one was to know
What's the purpose of their presence
Nor how far they would go.

Each time Liz tried to confront them
They simply drove away.
Not a word was ever spoken
As though nothing to say.

But soon after their departure
She saw they would return.
Assuming the same vantage point
To raise the same concern.

Everyone Has Their Secrets

While neither one wished to discuss
What if Gwen was to leave.
They had become like family
But neither was naïve.

It's clear that someone wanted Gwen
Who'd stoop to any mean
To find a way to get to her
Unless they intervene.

While everyone had their secrets,
Not all secrets were good.
So, Scott had needed to ask Gwen
If she had understood

There're people who wished to hurt her
Or to take her away.
While they would try to protect her
It may not be okay.

Did she know why they wanted her
Or could give them a clue
What purpose they may need her for
Or penalty was due?

Gwen's look had told them she'd no clue
To why she'd been pursued.
For she had been no one special
Why they'd want her subdued.

Scott had no choice but take her word
That she possessed no clue
To who may have wished to harm her
As nothing did she do.

THE DINNER

One night Liz took Gwen to dinner
As Scott was working late.
Scott had warned her not to do it
As Liz was tempting fate.

But Liz decided it's okay.
They'd be in public view.
There was no way they'd try something
If attention they drew.

They had just finished ordering
When two men had approached.
As neither Liz had recognized
She felt they had encroached.

While conversation meant for Liz,
Their eyes had not left Gwen.
Which gave Liz an eerie feeling
They'd chosen to close in.

Before Liz came to recognize
That they had clearly planned
To grab Gwen from the restaurant
And scrutiny withstand.

While one had made a play for Gwen,
The other restrained Liz.
Though both of them began to scream,
No one the act would quiz.

Though Liz could not believe it true
No challenge had been made.
For both of them had faced assault,
There's none who offered aid.

Then a waiter and a busboy
Had dared to intercede.
They saw two damsels in distress
And felt there was a need.

The men were taken by surprise
That any would fight back.
They had planned on no resistance
So, this was a setback.

When it seemed others may join in,
Both men chosen to run.
If Gwen was meant to be a prize,
It could not now be won.

The attack Liz thought was brazen
And not what she'd expect.
She thought the crowd brought protection
And, possibly, respect.

When Liz had gone to check on Gwen,
Gwen rudely pulled away.
For there clearly was a problem
As Gwen was not okay.

SCOTT'S RESPONSE

When Scott got word what had occurred
He had raced to the scene.
He must make sure they both were fine
Before Liz he'd demean.

For he'd told her not to do it
But warning she ignored.
Now she'd come close to losing Gwen
Which truly left him floored.

But once assured they were okay
He asked them what occurred.
Liz told him that they were attacked
But attack was deterred.

Yet, while Liz had been forthcoming,
Gwen, seemingly, had stewed.
It had been clear she was upset
And had been in a mood.

Then Scott asked for a description
Of how the men appeared.
So, he'd release a bulletin
Before they disappeared.

He thanked the waiter and busboy
Before Scott turned to leave.
He told them he was in their debt
For offering reprieve.

The other troopers mobilized
With manhunt to begin
For the two brazen miscreants
That Scott had wished to skin.

GWEN'S REACTION

It's clear that Gwen upset with Liz
As bedroom door she slammed.
They'd barely come into the house
And Liz already damned.

Liz had promised her protection
But that had been a lie.
Liz had chosen to expose her
But could not fathom why.

Gwen felt that she had been betrayed
And may well could have died.
The men were clearly after her
As caution not applied.

While Liz admitted her mistake
And forgiveness had asked.
Gwen had seemed to stand resolute
As anger was not masked.

It's something moms and daughters do
Was what Liz tried explain.
When Gwen's bedroom door thrown open
And forgiveness was plain.

THE MANHUNT

The manhunt had shown no results
As though both disappeared.
Which seemed unlikely without help
Which was what Scott had feared.

Someone had clearly wanted Gwen
Who would not be denied.
For attempts had seemed unending
In how hard they had tried.

The intrusions were unwelcomed
Though they seemed to persist.
As if they're coordinated
Despite how they'd resist.

The attempts had grown outrageous
In what they would pursue.
What was it that they wished of Gwen
That this they'd been put through.

DIRTY LOOKS

Liz had thought it was outrageous
Dirty looks Gwen still drew.
Her tenure Liz thought long enough
Where they had not been due.

If any of them got to know
The person Gwen had been.
The dirty looks would disappear
To not be seen again.

But not one of them had bothered
To with her have engaged.
Where they could find out for themselves
Their doubts could be assuaged.

So, the dirty looks continued
Though none of them were due.
They were just small-minded people
Who never thought things through.

EVERY OPTION

While every option was open
The option Scott would choose
Would be the one most dangerous
Where he had most to lose.

Since the manhunt unproductive,
He'd strike out on his own.
Where he'd seek the perpetrators
And bring them to atone.

He would search in his off-hours,
Though Liz he would not tell.
For he knew she would oppose it
And, maybe, give him hell.

John could read Scott like a novel
Where Scott's face told a tale.
Scott was planning something stupid
That may land him in jail.

John asked Scott what he was thinking
For his plan was insane.
He would be risking every thing
With little chance to gain.

He'd be turning vigilante
Where his badge he may lose.
He knew Liz would be against it
As this she'd not excuse.

It seemed Scott came to his senses
Taking John's words to heart.
It's a path he could not travel,
Thus, one he could not start.

That night when Scott had returned home,
He hugged both Liz and Gwen.
While rage still had burned within him
It's their love wished to win.

THE LIGHT

There were reports a light was seen
Stemming from the Wasteland.
Though Scott had been the first one there,
He failed to understand.

There was no light that he had seen,
Thus, thought a bogus call.
But there was a crowd that gathered
Who said they'd seen it all.

Each in the crowd had sworn to him
That they had seen the light.
Which, suddenly, had disappeared
Where once it had shone bright.

As though it knew Scott in approach
And presence wished to hide.
Some wondered what its purpose was
Though surely not to guide.

THE MISSING BOY

A young boy reported missing
Had put the town on edge.
His parents were beside themselves
With what they would allege.

It had to be a kidnapping
Of that they had been sure.
Their son was not a wanderer
As he was too mature.

Scott had been one of the troopers
Who to the scene was called.
The parents were hysterical
Though each detail recalled.

The troopers searched the area
Where some footprints were found
That had led into the Wasteland
Though that they thought profound.

For every child born in Winston
Taught from an early age
They were to avoid the Wasteland
And from it disengage.

Scott was intent in his pursuit
Of following the trail.
When his Sargent had intervened
To his pursuit derail.

For none allowed in the Wasteland
And that was by decree.
As the Wasteland was off-limits
Though Scott may disagree.

If the boy dared to wander in,
He had been lost for sure.
For the Wasteland unforgiving
Which no one could endure.

Perhaps he saw the Wasteland's lights
Which had served as a lure
That drew him past the danger point,
Beyond where he's secure.

His parents were devastated
When they received the news.
Their child was truly lost to them
Though truth they would refuse.

While Scott had found it difficult
To simply walk away.
The Sargent said he'd his reasons
Which Scott urged to obey.

THE MYSTERY OF THE WASTELAND

Scott turned to Liz seeking answers
As he'd not understood
The mystery of the Wasteland
And thought he never would.

The tales she told him, he dismissed,
As they could not be true.
But Liz had stared him in the eye
And said none were untrue.

Some had claimed that they'd seen movements
Sometimes at dusk or dawn.
But nothing had been clearly viewed
Where a conclusion drawn

She, too, had seen anomalies
Which she could not explain.
But they had frightened her enough
A distance she'd maintain.

The Wasteland was a mystery
That Scott could not explore.
For Liz had said it's no request
But something she'd implore.

For no one who had ventured in
Had been known to return.
The Wasteland was like a black hole,
Thus, her request was stern.

A Return to School

When Liz told Scott that she believed
That Gwen they should enroll.
Where she'd finish education
And could realize a goal.

Scott concerned about her safety
While she would be in school.
But Liz said there was a trooper
Where safety his to rule.

But school had proved a huge mistake
As no friends had she made.
Instead, she had been ostracized
And none came to her aid.

Gwen, clearly, had been viewed with scorn
Wherever she appeared.
Teenagers had made fun of her
Where some had even jeered.

The mystery surrounding her
Had sparked a sense of fear.
Who was found outside the Wasteland
Which no one would go near.

The fact that Gwen had grown sullen
Had told Liz something's wrong.
For Gwen was clearly not herself
As not upbeat and strong.

Liz went to see the principal
Where she'd lodge a complaint.
For her daughter had been bullied
From pictures she would paint.

Liz demanded that he stop it
Or she would rain down hell.
Once the School Board got wind of it
When tales she'd gladly tell.

Although he had tried to calm her,
He saw it of no use.
For she was beyond placating
And he had no excuse.

He promised her he'd intervene
And situation quelled.
Where for those who had persisted
He swore would be expelled.

THE KNOCK AT THE DOOR

A knock brought Liz to their front door
Where she was shocked to find
Two men who had been dressed in black
Whose entry she declined.

They asked if Gwen's available
To which Liz had replied
There was no Gwen at this address,
So, someone must have lied.

The men in black had not been fooled
As address was correct.
They'd watched the girl both come and go
As she'd been their subject.

The men in black had frightened Liz
Who're surely government.
Dark glasses were a giveaway
To why they had been sent.

She tried to close the door on them
But act had been denied.
It seemed no was not an answer
That they thought had applied.

THE MAN AT THE SCHOOL

The man who showed up at the school
Said he had come for Gwen.
He claimed he was a relative
But they'd not let him in.

The trooper came to question him
As entry was denied.
John said that Scott a friend of his
To which the man replied

That he was one of Scott's cousins
Who recently arrived.
He was looking to surprise Scott
Though that had seemed contrived.

John had chosen not to tell him
Elizabeth had called.
Who turned away two visitors
That had left her appalled.

John said Scott had not informed him
Someone's to pick up Gwen.
So, John must ask him for I.D.
To prove who he had been.

The man reached into his pocket
As if it to produce.
Then broke into an all-out sprint
Without a good excuse.

He jumped into a waiting car
Which next had sped away.
Another effort to grab Gwen
John feared he'd just delay.

CHERYL HARPER

Cheryl Harper had been new to town
Who had been ostracized.
The local kids tormented her
Where she was victimized.

Though Gwen had not defended her,
She did become her friend.
Where the two would commensurate
On what had been the trend.

The two of them were close in age
And status they had shared.
For neither one was popular
Though neither was impaired.

It was just they were outsiders
Which others won't accept.
So, they had formed their own circle
Where to themselves had kept.

THE ABDUCTION

Gwen's only friend was Cheryl Harper
Who, too, was new to town.
The other kids had ignored them
Or tried to put them down.

As they were walking home from school
The van they had ignored.
The threat was imperceptible,
So, it went unexplored.

He van that pulled up next to them
At first, caused no alarm.
Until two men had exited
And one grabbed Cheryl's forearm.

They drug the girl into the van
And then had sped away.
Leaving Gwen in a perplexed state
As exit she'd survey.

Gwen called police to summon aid
As Cheryl was kidnapped.
It all had happened so quickly
She had felt she was strapped.

Although police had questioned her
She'd little to relate.
Because both men had worn a mask
And terror had been great.

An office discovered Cheryl
On an abandoned road.
She told him a mistake was made
So, freedom was bestowed.

For the wrong girl had been taken.
As target had been Gwen.
The men simply apologized
Then winced in their chagrin.

Liz found Gwen was beside herself
To find mistake was made.
Gwen gladly would have gone with them
If she could make a trade.

THE CONFERENCE

When Gwen's teacher had approached Liz,
She, at first, was dismayed.
For she asked for a conference
So, status be relayed.

When Liz stepped into the classroom
She felt a sense of dread.
While she had no expectations
She feared what may be said.

Gwen's learning curve, remarkable,
Her teacher had began
But Gwen had some special issues
For which she could not plan.

She seemed to lack a foundation
Upon which she could build.
Though Gwen had been a quick learner
There're gaps that were not filled.

Liz told her they would work on things
With which she felt Gwen weak.
And try to bring her up to speed
Where issues they would tweak.

Gwen's teacher said she was relieved
That Liz took it so well.
As she'd heard with the principal
Liz rained on him pure hell.

GWEN'S PRIOR LIFE

Liz always found it curious
That Gwen could not recall
Any aspects of her childhood,
Not even glimpses small

Though it could be due to trauma
As nothing had they known
Of what had been Gwen's prior life
As it remained unknown.

She'd proved fiercely independent
As though she'd lived alone.
But Liz had thought it unlikely
Her age reached on her own.

But still it seemed mysterious
That Gwen could not reclaim
Any memory of childhood
Which Liz thought was a shame.

A SOCIAL LEPER

While Gwen knew about the parties
No invites she received.
For she'd been a social leper.
At least, what she perceived.

Although the taunting all but ceased,
She now had been ignored.
She found no place where she fit in
As she had been deplored.

Gwen had no clue to what she'd done
Where status was attained.
But the hallways were a gauntlet
Where contempt unrestrained.

While she lacked social acceptance
She found it was okay.
The time would come when they'd find need
And it would be her day.

AWARE OF SOCIAL ISSUES

Liz aware of social issues
With which Gwen made to deal.
But there was nothing she could do
To heighten Gwen's appeal.

If Gwen was given half a chance
Liz had been pretty sure
They'd find a friend that they could trust,
Whose friendship would endure.

She was plagued by misconceptions
Of who she'd truly been.
For none of them had took the time
To find out who was Gwen.

Although her heart went out to Gwen,
Liz could not intercede.
For that may clearly make things worse
And any chance impede.

Liz was ashamed she must admit
That when she had been young
The new kids' treatment was the same
Which now she knew had stung.

Liz hoped things would work out for Gwen
But having there been raised
She had found she's less than hopeful
A new trail would be blazed.

THE LIGHTS RETURN

It seemed the light appeared again
As switchboard had seemed crazed.
Reports came in from every where
But troopers seemed unfazed.

There had not been a schedule
To which it would adhere.
But it always drew attention
If not a sense of fear.

While the calls had been meaningless
As nothing could they do.
For the light had proven harmless
As far as any knew.

The only thing that seemed to change
Was this time there'd been two.
They said the lights were parallel
Which had been something new.

Although a ruckus had been raised
Once the lights came to fade
Every thing returned to normal
Where no concern displayed.

THE ASSAULT

Scott caught a call of an assault
But found when he arrived
A woman, a man had restrained
Which seemed the call contrived.

He said her name was Lilly Rose
Who he thought lost her mind.
She tried to enter the Wasteland
As to the threat seemed blind.

His efforts made to save her life
Not to see her done in.
For if she entered the Wasteland
She'd not be seen again.

Scott, too, had thought it had been strange
That she had seemed possessed.
As it had seemed with the Wasteland
The woman seemed obsessed.

Scott tried to calm the woman down
But met with no success.
It seemed her mind had been made up
As no fear she'd express.

Then, suddenly, she calmed herself
As if woke from a trance.
Where she questioned why Scott was called,
Tossing a second glance.

While the man who had restrained her
Had simply disappeared.
Perhaps to let Scott handle it
Or an arrest had feared.

The woman then excused herself
To set about her way.
Without any indication
She tried to herself slay.

What Scott had come to recognize
Each time the light appeared
It's followed by an incident
That seemed extremely weird.

PROM

When Gwen invited to the prom,
Politely she declined.
For she feared it was a setup
With what may be designed.

But an invite Cheryl accepted
In hope her status changed.
She saw a night that's magical
That had not been arranged.

Although Gwen had tried to warn her,
Gwen's warnings were ignored.
Cheryl thought that Gwen had grown
       jealous
So, had not been on board.

The prom was an embarrassment
That Cheryl walked into.
For she'd been humiliated
Which, clearly, was not due.

She had only sought acceptance
Which she thought she had won.
Just to find she's disrespected
As of her they made fun.

They laughed as she had fled the gym
And tears had filled her eyes.
They thought she brought it on herself
To think that she they'd prize.

Gwen tried her best to comfort her
As Cheryl was truly hurt.
For that was what a friend would do
Where pain she'd try divert.

DARK ELEMENTS

As John had pulled Scott to the side,
Scott saw John was concerned.
For something clearly bothered him
As to whispers he turned.

There seemed to be dark elements
Beyond the ones they'd known.
Whose motives were ulterior
Beyond what had been shown.

There had been much more at stake
Than any of them knew.
The girl had been the centerpiece
But to what, he'd no clue.

The Wasteland not the only thing
That seemed to be amiss.
The agents and the eerie light
He found he can't dismiss.

Whether all of them related
Or each was its own threat.
There, clearly, were dark elements
That, so far, went unmet.

THE SHUNNING

It had been quite by accident
Liz noticed she was shunned.
As everyone had passed her by
Which left her truly stunned.

For no one would acknowledge her
Nor greeting would return.
As though she had ceased to exist
Which had caused her concer.

Even the supermarket clerks
Refused to speak to her.
Which had almost been unheard of
That clerks would not confer.

Although she found it difficult
With it she'd gladly deal.
As she thought it Gwen related
The pain she would conceal.

If the people that small-minded
Then they could go to hell.
She would not turn her back on Gwen
Despite what they may shell.

TO PROVE HIM WRONG

Scott had begged Liz to prove him wrong
That there's not something more
To why these men were stalking Gwen
As if a prize to score.

She seemed to be a wayward child
As far as Scott had known.
Perhaps a child that wandered off
Where no love had been shown.

Though he'd felt pretty confident
Nothing illegal done.
Otherwise, there'd be a warrant
Where options they'd have none.

The men in black would indicate
The government involved.
But why was Gwen of interest
A riddle he'd not solved.

Scott worried that the day would come
When they'd, somehow, succeed
In taking Gwen away from them
As nothing's guaranteed.

For they were merely citizens
Who faced a government
That was not always forthcoming
In nature of intent.

RUNAWAY

While Gwen had come to love them both,
Her presence took a toll.
For she'd seen how they'd been treated
Which would eat at her soul.

When Liz had called Gwen to dinner,
No response had been drawn.
So, Liz had gone to look for her
To find that Gwen was gone.

Gwen had grown to understand
The problem had been her.
It's she who'd drawn the dirty looks
And what they would infer.

She left behind a note for them
With thanks for all they'd done.
But she had caused them so much pain
She felt the need to run.

While Liz grew frantic from the note
As it had caught her blind.
In panic she had next called Scott
As kept presence of mind.

Though Scott told her not to worry
As he would look for Gwen.
He could tell his wife on the verge
Of a total tailspin.

Scott found her at the bus station
Where hoodie worn to hide
The visage of identity,
So, no one would deride.

When Scott sat down right next to her,
She barely looked around.
Then he asked for destination
If any she had found.

He told her that she could not run
From every problem faced.
Sometimes she had to make a stand
And for response be braced.

She knew she was responsible
For troubles they had known.
She saw that people turned on them
As that was clearly shown.

She wanted to unburden them
From what they had been through.
She thought it best that she should leave
As happiness they're due.

The sacrifices that they made
To Gwen went well beyond
For a stranger that they'd taken in
And with whom tried to bond.

Then Scott replied it had been her
That brought to them great joy.
It's time that both of them go home
Where Liz they could annoy.

A REAPPEARANCE
OF THE LIGHT

The light, again, had reappeared
But this time seemed to move.
Both John and Scott arrived on scene
So sight they could disprove.

But both of them had seen the light
Which had an eerie glow.
Neither one had believed their eyes
But knew that it was so.

Both questioned what the light had meant,
For it must mean something.
But natives had been hesitant
To admit anything.

They turned to find John Smith was there
Who, clearly, saw the light.
He looked as though he'd seen a ghost
As eyes reflected fright.

They wished to ask him what he knew
But he had disappeared.
He, somehow, simply slipped away
As quiet as appeared.

John said that they should track him down
To find out what he knew.
But Scott replied there was no use
As answers would be few.

OLD MAN WILSON

Old man Wilson had gone missing,
Or so, his neighbors said.
For they'd not seen a trace of him
And feared he may be dead.

When Scott had rolled up to his house
There'd been no sign he'd seen
That would point to a disturbance
Where he should intervene.

They said he was a scientist
Who recently retired.
And he had proved a lovely man
Who lives greatly inspired.

While he may have had his secrets
Of them he had kept mum.
He never spoke about his work
But when asked would turn glum.

There're none who said they'd seen something
That had seemed out of place.
Old man Wilson simply vanished
Which they found a disgrace.

HOW THE WASTELAND VIEWED

The Wasteland had a hold on them
It seemed none could resist.
As though it was a living thing
That through them would exist.

Their fear was almost reverence
In how it had been viewed.
As though it was omnipotent
And through it they're renewed.

While the people were terrorized
The Wasteland they'd embrace.
For it gave them identity
They'd chosen to retrace.

For the Wasteland born of secrets
That no one wished revealed.
Where the secrets now were precious
And had to be concealed.

They thought it was beyond the truth
In what inside it laid.
Where, while they may have worshipped it,
Of it they were afraid.

THE MEN IN BLACK RETURN

Liz noticed that the men in black
Made a silent return.
She saw them parked across the street
Which made her anger burn.

They seemed to think they were stealthy
But that was not the case.
For any fool could clearly see
That they looked out of place.

Why could they not be left alone
Devoid of scrutiny?
They had nothing to offer them
Except anxiety.

Why was it Gwen so great a prize
Harassment was in vogue?
Did they think Gwen was an agent
Who'd suddenly gone rogue?

Perhaps, she thought, she should call Scott
But if he got involved.
She feared what he may choose to do
If issue not resolved.

She could have tried chase them away
But what good would that do?
Another group would take their place
Where stakeout they'd renew.

Then Liz had gone to check on Gwen
To made sure she's okay.
Liz saw no need to worry Gwen
With what she'd just survey.

MISSING

When Liz had gone to check on Gwen,
She found that Gwen was gone.
Her bedroom window had been smashed
Where one conclusion drawn.

In total panic Liz called Scott
To tell him Gwen was gone.
It seemed someone had taken her
At some point before dawn.

Her bedroom window had been smashed
As though someone broke in
And forcibly had taken her
Was what had been her spin.

Liz said he had to look for her,
Though may be hard to find.
She'd no clue who had taken her,
At least, that came to mind.

Scott said he thought he may have known
What this had been about.
But it laid within the Wasteland
And of that had no doubt.

A MIND MADE UP

When Scott came home, he was on fire
As anger burned within.
For Gwen was taken from their home
Which he viewed as a sin.

Liz asked him what he planned to do
But response greatly feared.
He had not seemed to be himself
Which had to Liz seemed weird.

Scott said he's going after her
And the risks could be damned.
For their daughter had been taken
As duffle bad was crammed.

Scott grabbed his rifle and his gun
As he was mad as hell.
Elizabeth had cried and pleaded
In fear this won't end well.

Then grabbed a bag from their closet
That Scott brought home from war.
Liz had no clue what it contained
Nor what it had been for.

While Scott was clear in his intent
Where Wasteland he'd invade.
For he was going after Gwen
Despite what price he paid.

Though Liz had begged him not to go
As both she could not lose.
It's clear his mind had been made up
As reason he'd refuse.

SCOTT'S FIRST STOP

Scott's first stop was to see John Smith
To find what he had known
Of what the Wasteland may contain
And, thus, to pick his brain.

It was clear that he knew something
The others had not known.
Scott wanted to know everything
As it he'd face alone.

John Smith had tried to ward Scott off
As answers were denied.
But Scott was growing adamant
That answers be supplied.

For his daughter had been taken
Who he meant to retrieve.
If Smith would not cooperate,
The feat may not achieve.

Smith saw that Scott was desperate
Which he knew a bad sign.
For desperation can lead to
A crossing of the line.

While Smith was clearly hesitant,
Scott saw there're things he knew.
Which Scott would acquire forcibly
If that's what it came to.

The old man said follow the light
To where it had been seen.
But he must proceed with caution
For the land could be mean.

For there were things in the Wasteland
That nightmares would contain.
He cannot pause or hesitate
But pace he must maintain.

SOMETHING IN THE WASTELAND

A few miles into the Wasteland
Scott stopped to take a rest.
While he tried to get his bearings,
He'd grown to feel unrest.

There seemed something in the Wasteland
That had not been defined.
For there're questions without answers
That any were to find.

The missing boy and incursions
Both seemed a senseless act.
As though something in the Wasteland
Would from the town extract.

Scott could feel it was watching him
In effort to decide
If Scott had been worth attacking
Or from Scott it should hide.

Although to Scott invisible
Its presence he could feel.
Scott brought his gun to the ready
Believing the threat real.

While Scott had feared he's overmatched
He would not turn away.
For he had come to reclaim Gwen
And won't deal with delay.

THE JOURNEY

While the darkness of the Wasteland
Had sparked in Scott true fear.
He swore he'd see the mission through
Despite what may appear.

For the Wasteland a mystery
Of which few dared to speak.
Scott was unsure what he may face
As the land appeared bleak.

There was no way Scott gives her up
No matter what the stakes.
For Gwen had been like family
And would do what it takes.

For periods the light he'd see
But it would come and go.
So, the course that he had plotted
Had forced him to go slow.

The darkness made it difficult
For him to find his way.
As he constantly had stumbled
Where for each fall he'd pay.

For his legs were bruised and bleeding
Where one began to swell.
Although his progress had been slowed
He'd not wish Gwen farewell.

THE SECRET OF THE WASTELAND

He had considered giving up
As he was wracked with pain.
For both legs he found were injured
And pants red with blood stain.

Scott then saw the Wasteland's secret
Which had filled him with awe.
It was a huge facility
Where he had dropped his jaw.

He wondered how much Smith had known
And had he'd been involved.
He, at least once, must have seen it
As to it seemed resolved.

It jutted from the barren land
As though placed there by God.
While a fence had surrounded it
Which to Scott had seemed odd.

There'd been little to threaten it
As far as Scott had known.
It seemed that such security
May have been overblown.

Guards patrolled the perimeter,
So, entry not assured.
But Scott determined to get in
Though pathway seemed obscured.

THE BREAK-IN

Scott waited for the guards to pass
Then had dashed for the door.
He'd not known what may lay inside
But driven to explore.

Once entry made, he hugged the walls
So, he would not be seen.
Though based on the activity
His presence seemed routine.

The place had been a busy hub
With people everywhere.
Where there seemed there's little notice
That he was even there.

The Wasteland hid a biolab
As all had been deceived.
It may have been a barren land
But secrecy achieved.

He surveyed the interior
Where Wilson he had seen.
As it appeared he was involved
In this strange mystery.

The funding that the place required
Had almost blown his mind.
It must be astronomical
The way it was designed.

A platform Gwen had occupied
To whom sensors attached.
While he knew it would be risky
A wild plan he had hatched.

While men in black surrounded it,
Scott firmly had believed
That if he had proved quick enough
Rescue could be achieved.

Gwen looked as though a Guinea pig
The way she was displayed.
Where Scott's anger again surfaced
That Gwen they would degrade.

About to make a dash for Gwen
When the alarms would sound.
Where armed guards had surrounded him
As his presence was found.

Scott surrendered rather quickly
As he'd no wish to die.
There was no way that he could win
If bullets were to fly.

After assured Scott was no threat
A man slowly approached.
Who told him that he was impressed
How he the lab had broached.

While he had admired Scott's courage,
It all had been for naught.
For, now, that he had seen the place
The penalty he'd wrought

Was a life of isolation
As he could not reveal
The fact of the facility
They'd worked hard to conceal.

Those they found within the Wasteland
Were captured and secured.
For the secrets of the Wasteland
They must assure endured.

Scott replied they could not keep him
Even if they should dare.
For he'd taken some precautions
That they should be aware.

He also said he would not leave
If Gwen not by his side.
For he had come to bring her home
And would not be denied.

For he had planted transmitters
To serve him as a guide
As he exited the Wasteland
With Gwen close by his side.

They worked on special frequencies
Which they would never find.
Though he promised to remove them
Where none be left behind.

But warned them if they're not released
He had left with a friend
A second device to track them
If they should not ascend.

The man replied it was a trick
But he would not be played.
Scott replied he's not a prankster
And threat was no charade.

He asked Scott why he wanted Gwen.
What had she been to him?
For she served no earthly purpose
But satisfy a whim.

Gwen was a lab experiment
Whose results would exceed
Even wildest expectations
In how well they'd succeed.

She was conceived in a test tube
Then by them had been raised.
They'd not thought of her as human
But as new path they blazed.

She may have been man's creation
But daughter she'd become.
He'd not leave the place without her
Nor to his threats succumb.

Scott had found he was dumbfounded
When Gwen was heard to say
She may be an experiment
But did not wish to stay.

While she's the first one of her kind
She wished life to explore.
Not subject to experiments
Where desires would ignore.

All she wanted was live a life
Where she would come to know
What it meant to be a human
And have a chance to grow.

She had grown disoriented
Once her escape was made.
She'd never been outside the lab
Where she had grown afraid.

That's when Scott had discovered her
And chose to take her in.
He and his wife had cared for her,
And gave her the name Gwen.

When the man who wore the lab coat
Was by a guard approached.
Who had confirmed what Scott had said
Their privacy was poached.

There, apparently, were sensors
That they could not locate.
For Scott had a couple on him
Which they could simulate.

Though the man grew aggravated,
He found his hands were tied.
For it was the facility
To which he had been tied.

Its secrecy must be assured
So, if Scott gave his word
He said he'd order their release
Which, up to now, unheard.

As they were leaving Scott remarked
If they were not aware.
There was something in the Wasteland
Of which they should beware.

They removed each of the sensors
As they made their way out.
For Scott had given them his word
And to it was devout.

Scott was careful when they emerged,
That they had not been seen.
Though the secrets of the Wasteland
He thought to be obscene.

There'd been much more to the Wasteland
Than the facility.
For there were other incidents
That heightened mystery.

When they emerged, John was waiting
Who asked them what they seen.
Where Scott had merely shook his head
As answer he must screen.

As Scott stared at its emptiness,
A poem he recalled.
That had spoken of the Wasteland
Which now left him appalled.

ODE TO THE WASTELAND

When we wander through the Wasteland
What do we hope to find?
For the Wasteland is desolate,
Uncaring and unkind.

While the Wasteland full of mystery,
Strange danger and deceit.
It's true once the Wasteland entered
One finds there's no retreat.

It seemed an evil entity
Devoid of heart and soul.
The harshness of reality
That has only one goal.

To enslave those who are foolish
To think they are aware
The Wasteland a sanctuary
When in truth, would ensnare.

GWEN'S RETURN

Gwen welcomed home with open arms
As Liz began to cry.
She thought that Gwen was gone for good
And had not said goodbye.

They told Liz of their adventure,
Though some details left out.
But many stories Liz had missed
As Gwen would also spout.

Liz found she was flabbergasted
To learn that Gwen could speak.
Where her heart had begun to race
And knees seemed to grow weak.

Scott told Liz of Gwen's origin
Though neither truly cared.
For to them she was their daughter
Who with them life had shared.

Gwen was the valedictorian
While Cheryl was number two.
Though were banned from social circles
They'd more time for review.

Both of then became college grads
Though ways they came to part.
As both had diff'rent ambitions
That seemed to claim each heart.

Gwen had married a lovely man,
To whom three children born.
Liz and Scott became grandparents
Whose pride had been well worn.

Scott and Liz had kept Gwen's secret
Until the day they died.
While Gwen had mourned the both of them
For love they had supplied.